CW0086498

New Adages

Volume 1

Our Mission

We believe that life is a conversation and if you approach all of life's interactions as conversations, you remove fear and open up possibility.

We believe that no matter your financial situation, you are entitled to information that will change your life for the better.

We have a passionate spirit and a lofty goal: to change the way people talk to each other.

We believe that talking never makes things worse.

We believe there is no such thing as a bad conversation.

We believe in speaking your truth.

We believe in starting conversations (and starting them when issues are small).

We will empower you with the tools and knowledge you need to change the conversation.

The Kindred Conversation
Start a conversation. Change your life.

What are the New Adages?

An adage is a short saying that transmits knowledge, and some have been around for generations. You might remember a parent or grandparent saying: "A bird in the hand is worth two in the bush", "A leopard can't change its spots", or "Better safe than sorry." There are hundreds of these sayings and they all translate into excellent advice and food for thought.

I have come up with dozens of new adages over the years. Some are quotes from famous people, some I heard somewhere and they stuck with me, and others I just made up.

We all know how difficult it can be to learn a new behavior. Throughout my practice I have used the new adages to help my clients. They serve as prompts to actions or self checking. Many new adages are interconnected, but they are meant to be explored in any order, and revisited frequently.

I have had clients that I saw 25 years ago tell me that not only do they still use the new adages, but many people in their lives use them as well. It is my sincere hope that these ideas have the same effect in your life.

– Karen

How to use this book

We all have automatic thoughts that we repeat to ourselves over and over again. This makes our neurons fire in a certain way. When we change those thoughts from negative to positive, the old neurons die, and new ones are created.

The New Adages can take over old negative thoughts and actions, and change the way you think and respond to external events, as well as your own moods and feelings. Mindfulness made easy.

The best way to utilize this book is to first read through the entire book, which takes about 30 minutes. Take note as you're reading which adages really resonate with you. Pick one adage and use it. Read it in the morning and at night. Turn it over in your mind. Think of times it would've helped you in the past.

Use the adage as an affirmation. Talk about it with friends and colleagues. Watch and be aware. When you are at a crossroads, this adage will actually put you into mindfulness, and will alter your old ways of doing things.

We don't need to reinvent the wheel again, but we can find new and different ways to use it.

New Adages Volume 1

W.A.I.T.
(Why am I talking?)

I heard this saying at a conference and it reminded me of something my sister told me years ago. She had moved to a new town and said that whenever she was stopped at a red light and it turned green she counted to three before she started to go again. This was a precaution she developed by noticing how many people ran red lights there.

If we all counted to three before we opened our mouths, made a decision, or got angry, we would save ourselves a lot of pain. Counting to three doesn't take very long — but it's enough time to pause and think and positively change an outcome.

Look at it as a way for you to quickly contemplate what you are about to say. Do you really need to say it, or text it, or tweet it for that matter? Will it really matter or will it just make things worse? Think about the sleepless nights you've had worrying about something you said during the day. Take those few seconds to ask yourself "Why am I talking?"

Life is a conversation.

The first thing that comes to mind when we say the word "communicate" or "let's talk" is usually "ohhhhh no!!!"

As the years have gone by I have witnessed so many people in my office trying to learn to "communicate". And most of the time it's horrible. There are so many rules, roles, and ways to "communicate" that it is virtually impossible to really listen and converse.

Rather than thinking of an unpleasant topic as a confrontation or communication (ugh), change it in your mind to a conversation. When we approach one another using the word conversation it just sets up the situation in a more casual way. There are some conversations that are more difficult than others but they are still just conversations!

Take the fear out of starting an exchange. Just have a conversation.

Speak your truth.

The truth is very interesting — there is your truth, my truth and THE truth. All feelings are real to the individual feeling them; however, this does not make them true in the outer world. In order to be healthy and happy, we first need to realize that our feelings are not facts: they are feelings.

One of the biggest excuses I hear to not speak our truth is that it won't matter. The other person won't get it, and they will do what they want anyway. Speaking your truth is all about knowing yourself well enough to make sense of how you feel and then having the self esteem and respect to say what is on your mind and in your heart. If you don't let others know how you feel and what you need, they can't give you those things or at least negotiate with you.

The only obligation you have in any relationship is to let someone know how you feel, what you want, and where you are coming from. In other words: speak your truth!

Response-ability.

The word RESPONSIBILITY can be confusing. Most of us look at it as kind of a negative. We see it as something that we have to do, an obligation — heavy and serious. We NEED to be responsible, we HAVE to take care of things, people, tasks, etc. It feels like a weight on our backs and our minds.

I am going to give you another way to define responsibility: THE ABILITY TO RESPOND.

Whenever something happens to us, either expected or out of the blue, we always have the ability to respond. So don't think of responsibility as "taking on something", think of it as "responding to something".

We always have choices and we can take a minute to look over our options and decide how to respond. That decision is not only the ACTION we take, but how we choose to FEEL about it.

When something does happen, accept that maybe there isn't anything you can do about it. If you CAN do something about it, the time to respond is right THEN! Figure out what you need to do about it, how you're going to feel about it and move on.

Let them know, then let it go.

We all need to speak our truth. This simply means that no one can read our minds. It doesn't matter if you have been married for 50 years, or dated someone for 10 months. You have to assume that the other party has no clue as to how you feel, what you need, or what you want. It is your responsibility to let them know!!

When we are communicating with another person it is not our job to determine how they are going to respond to us. Think about it like a tennis match – you don't serve the ball to the other court and then run over there to return the shot the way you want it returned. You need to deal with what is returned to you.

Here's how a conversation might flow:
"You seem upset, but you told me you weren't upset with me so I'm letting it go. I'm choosing to believe you. If that's not the case, I guess you'll tell me later."

Let them know, and then let it go.

Almost nothing is about you.

When someone is acting different around us, we often assume that we have done something to make them upset with us. Typically when we ask, we find out that they are hungry, or tired, or had a stressful day, or had a fight with someone.

Guess what? Almost nothing is about you! You're just not that important. This might sound harsh, but you'll find it is actually a relief!

If someone around you is upset, take one of two approaches, and save yourself a lot of stress and time spent worrying about other people's problems:

1. Assume that it is not about you, because almost nothing is about you. Don't worry about it and wait for the other party to speak their truth. If it is indeed about you, have a conversation about it.

2. Let them know, and let it go. We can always ask if something is wrong, but when we do, we absolutely have to believe what the other party says.

The three f's: firm, fair, and friendly.

This is a simple guide to communicating in an assertive manner. Many times we shut down and say nothing because we are afraid of a confrontation with someone. If we learn to be FIRM, FAIR, and FRIENDLY we can take some of the fear out of confrontation.

FIRM

Know exactly what you need, communicate it clearly, and have solid boundaries.

FAIR

Don't ask someone to do something that we ourselves wouldn't do.

FRIENDLY

Say it in a friendly manner – this includes your tone of voice and nonverbal behavior.

BYOB: be in your own business.

Your family, friend's or acquaintance's personal issues (money, their relationships, their work issues, anything that does not involve you personally) are NONE of your business.

Yes, you read that right: NONE OF YOUR BUSINESS.

Think about how many times a day, week, or month, that you are upset about someone else's problems. I'll bet it is more often then you realize!

BYOB. Be in Your Own Business. This simply means that if it doesn't affect you then stay out of it. This keeps life simple.

When you find yourself engaged in other people's problems, ask yourself: "Does this particular issue have anything to do with me?" "Can I fix it?" "Can I change anything about my behavior that will help?" "Is there any way I can truly help this person?"

And, perhaps the most important question: "Is this any of my business?"

Better or worse?

When you do something that you are not quite sure about, stop for a moment after and ask yourself "do I feel better or do I feel worse?"

As you quickly think about this, the answer is usually very clear and direct. You then need to make a mental note about how that action made you feel, and move on. It is surprising how deeply this little phrase affects your future actions and thoughts. This gets you in touch with that still inner voice we all have, that truly knows us and has our best interests at heart.

By saying "better or worse?" often, and not overthinking whatever we did, be it an action, a comment or a thought, we create a new thought pattern that replaces the old one. And remember, when you change your thinking, you change your life.

No expectations.

Research has shown that people who don't have expectations are the happiest people. This does NOT mean that you settle for things. We all deserve to be treated well and to have quality in our lives; however, when we have expectations about how someone should treat us, or how some external event should turn out, we are setting ourselves up for disappointment. So don't settle and don't expect, you'll be a much happier person for that!

Stimulus 2, response 10.

Let's say there was a scale from 1 to 10 with 1 being "no big deal" and 10 being "total freak out." Essentially, 'Stimulus 2, response 10' is when something happens that is in reality a 2 and your response or the response that you get from your partner is at a level 10. A complete overreaction, and totally out of proportion to the thing that happened. The situation becomes totally unproductive and there is no hope for a conversation.

Stimulus 2, response 10 is a bit like post traumatic stress. When something brings up feelings for us that have been there in the past, those feelings are amplified through cellular memory, creating a much greater response to the stimuli than is appropriate.

So how do you keep yourself from blowing things out of proportion?

1. Address things when they are small, with the appropriate level response. When the stimulus is 2, respond at 2 and respond quickly. Don't let a situation linger until it becomes something bigger than it should be.

2. If you sense that you're blowing something out of proportion. Stop. Just stop and take a moment to dial your reaction back to an appropriate level. This will start to come more naturally over time, but the first step is just being aware of your reaction and mindful of whether or not you're at the appropriate level.

3. And if you're on the receiving end, remember that 99% of the time, it's not about you. When your partner is upset, quiet, stressed, or angry, (or conversely, when your partner is happy or excited), it's really not about you. Sorry. But it's not. So try to find out what is REALLY going on so that it doesn't escalate. Or don't. Because it's not about you anyway.

Lose a different way.

Years ago I played league tennis and I lost every match. Not 6-0, 6-0, but after playing for HOURS and losing in tie-breakers. My husband told me what a coach once said to him:

"Lose a different way."

If I was going to lose anyway, why not change up my game? I've since realized that this works well in life, not just tennis.

Think about it, if you are unhappy in a situation — be it a relationship, work or any other place — if you're experiencing something in your life that is causing you stress or conflict: change up your game. What harm will it do to change your approach overtly as well as internally? This is such a great way of taking the fear and risk out of changing your behavior.

We are all afraid to switch our game up because we might lose. We don't realize that we are already losing. When you lose a different way, you will actually start winning because the pressure and fear are gone.

Don't keep doing the same thing over and over again. The worst thing that will happen is that you'll still lose. But, I can pretty much guarantee it will get better. You will start to win simply by changing your thinking.

"It's easier to stay out than get out."

— Mark Twain

This is one of my most favorite quotes and should be a filter for almost all of the decisions you make in life. It simply means to think before you speak or act, consider the ramifications, and then proceed with caution.

It is so much harder to talk your way out of something, or get out of something that you committed to, than it is to just stay out of it in the first place.

Change your thinking, change your life.

This has been the theme of my practice since the beginning and it is one of the most powerful concepts I try to ingrain in each of my clients.

Every thought creates a feeling, which in turn creates an action. Imagine the power of creating the thought that could determine how you wanted to feel, despite the external environment!

You have a choice. Start to remind yourself that you have a choice. You make the weather. You have total control over your thoughts. It's just a matter of talking to yourself.

Is it simple? Yes. Is it easy? No. But when you start to do it, you'll never go back.

Stop forecasting, you're not a meteorologist.

In relationships, forecasting is when you think about (and worse, **talk about**) how the relationship will end up on your first or second date -- or in extreme cases, even before you go out! Could I marry this person? Could I have children with this person? Etc. You look into the future and predict all sorts of things, and I've found that most of the time, the forecast is negative.

Remember, forecasting is not a science and there is a large margin of error. When you forecast you scare yourself, you scare the person you are dating and you might lose out on a great relationship.

First and foremost, don't spend too much time forecasting and expecting terrible things to happen. You'll then emotionally live through it when most of the time it never happens. That is really not very smart, because you are suffering needlessly!

STOP FORECASTING. Live in the moment you are in.

Whatever you put your attention on expands.

Whenever you experience something, interpersonally or otherwise, you can spin it any way you choose. The story you tell yourself about it becomes your truth and you can tell that story in a negative or positive way.

Just like a politician, we spin things. Without the skills to know how to spin things in a positive light, we lie in darkness, which is always scary.

We as human beings tend to confirm our bias. When we perceive that things will turn out a certain way, or people will behave a certain way, we start to focus on the assumed outcome and we actually make it happen because that is what we are paying attention to!

This is the power of your attention. Your energy. Whatever you put your attention on, your energy on, EXPANDS. It happens. Thoughts + attention + energy + action = outcome.

You choose where to put your attention.
Choose wisely.
Choose to assume good intent in other people.
Above all else, choose positivity.

Start when things are small.

When dealing with issues in a relationship it is always easier to start to address issues when they are small. By this I mean: speak your truth as soon as something bothers you. If you have a conversation at the beginning of an issue, you can can deal with it more effectively.

It's kind of like when you see your closet getting messy. You watch it and think: "I really should organize." Instead, you just pack in more stuff and close the door. Eventually, you can't even open your closet without being overwhelmed and anxious! If you would have just folded that sweater and hung up that pair of pants in the first place, you'd have a much smaller problem!

When someone does something you don't like, or hurts your feelings, if you don't let them know right away, they will probably keep doing it. This can go on for years! And the hurt feelings build and build and finally you freak out. The other party in the relationship will probably be surprised – the usual response is: "What's your problem?" You have to backtrack, explain, give examples and get way too upset! The other person also gets upset because, while this has been going on for years to you, it is seemingly coming out of nowhere for them.

See, isn't this a lot more work than if you had just said something the first time it happened? Stay mindful, be in the here and now, and nip these unpleasant situations in the bud!

That which is squelched is not dead.

When we don't speak our truth and let others know how we feel and what we need and want, we are making a HUGE mistake. When we suppress our thoughts and feelings, they do not go away. They fester inside and become toxic. Little things become big things. It is then that people become passive aggressive! This is one of the ugliest forms of communication. It is so **so SO** detrimental to a relationship.

That which is squelched is not dead. Yes, I said it again and I can't emphasize this enough. If you don't take care of it it will come out in another way, whether that is aggressive or passive aggressive interactions, or in self-medication through eating, drinking, and/or drugs.

It is critical that you speak your truth, and speak it often.

The only person you can control is you.

It's time to let go of the notion that you have any control over another person. The only person you can control is you. The paradox of control is, the more I try and control you, the more you are actually controlling me.

What good does it do for you to get wrapped around an axle if you can't do anything about it? The only thing you can do is to find a different way to deal with it. You can't make someone or a situation change. Change yourself or your reaction. Find a different way.

If you don't ask, you don't get.

A lot of my clients feel defeated. Shut out of conversations, opportunities, choices, and experiences. When I probe into these feelings of defeat, I find that a lot of times they haven't even asked for what they want.

If you don't ask, you don't get! Never assume the answer is 'no'. (And really, being told 'no' is the worst thing that could happen, and that's not that bad.)

Think about it this way: if you don't ask, the answer is always 'no'.

Always ask. At the very least it is a starting point for negotiation.

A change is as good as a rest.

This is one of my favorite adages, because nothing is more constant in life than change. And the way you think about change will become the way you react to changes in your life.

A lot of my clients get very stressed out about changes — job changes, relationship changes, life changes. Some changes you can control, and some you can't control, but I think you should look at change as a positive thing either way.

In fact, if you're feeling tired of your life — proactively look at ways of changing it. These could be major things — like ending a bad relationship or pursuing a different career path, but even little changes can be as beneficial as taking a vacation.

Order something different at the coffee shop, take the train instead of driving, check out a yoga class instead of going for a run. One of two things will happen — your new choice will bring you new joy, or it will make you appreciate your old choice. And sometimes we need to make little changes to trust that the big changes will also be beneficial to us, even when they scare us a bit.

"The best place to start is to start."

There is a reason this quote has survived 26 centuries. It is one of the most powerful ideas in existence, and something I frequently bring up with my clients, who are often overwhelmed by the situations in which they find themselves.

I think of it this way:
The only thing you know for sure is the past.
You don't know the future.
You're existing in the present.

You can always pivot. You can always change course. But if you don't get started, nothing will ever change.

The best place to start is just to start because you know it.
You're here.
Right now.
Get started.

Don't be the drama.

I've created a new word: dramatizing.

Dramatizing: When an individual puts their own spin on any given situation, thereby creating drama.

Dramatizing occurs when the individual actually believes their perception is reality.

Drama can end up being much worse than trauma because it is largely made up in the mind of the person, whereas trauma is a real thing that can be dealt with.

Whenever you feel dramatized just ask yourself: Is it real? Or is it drama? 99% of the time it is drama, and guess what, 99% of the time it's NOT ABOUT YOU. Forget about it and move on!

The best defense to dramatizing is knowing how you think and perceive the situation, and being confident in your assessment of the situation.

And most importantly: **don't be the drama.**

Authenticity doesn't always work.

The mantra for most of us is "be authentic" — find your true self and discover who you truly are. Look, self discovery is important. I'm not saying that authenticity is not a valuable goal — but how is that working for you?

I've been reading more about Chinese wisdom, and discovered that the contemporary emphasis on self-discovery and authenticity may have really messed with all of us.

Instead of struggling to be authentic, Confucius suggested we try another approach: 'AS IF...' rituals. These 'AS IF...' rituals can help us break out of our own reality for a moment. We break from who we are when we see we are in unproductive patterns we have created, and actively work to shift them — AS IF we were different people in the moment. These rituals are actually the opposite of authenticity, that's what makes them work.

If you have pattern of relating to someone, change it up! These don't have to be massive changes. Let's say you never make the bed, and it's constantly a source of frustration. So you decide to get up in the morning AS IF you are a person that makes the bed! You make the bed and see how that changes your relationship. You would be surprised how little changes like this can make a big impact.

Stop going to the B.A.R.

Bitterness, Anger, Resentment. These are the most damaging emotions we can take with us after being hurt. The B.A.R. is a very negative place to be.

Many things don't turn out the way we would like. Relationships end, and we have all been treated badly at one time or another. This is true not only in affairs of the heart but also with relatives, friends, children, siblings, coworkers, etc. There are skills you can learn that will help you avoid bitterness, anger and resentment.

Mindfulness: When we practice mindfulness, we learn to feel those ugly emotions, examine them, then let go of them. We don't keep ruminating over them. Some the most important skills you can use come from mindfulness.

Almost nothing is about you: One of the best ways to avoid the B.A.R. is to remember that ALMOST NOTHING IS ABOUT YOU. The decisions people make are their decisions. The consequences do affect you, however you cannot control what someone else does.

Whatever you put your attention on expands: You may feel like going to the B.A.R. The pull may prove irresistible. Stay for a minute but quickly move on so those negative feelings don't get bigger.

Let them know and let it go: Be sure to have that conversation with the person that has hurt you. Then you have done your part and the rest is up to them.

You are in control of you: Remember that how YOU deal with these issues will mostly affect you, and you are in control of you!

About us

Karen Kindred, LCSW

Karen Kindred specializes in individual and couples therapy, and maintains a private practice in Salt Lake City, Utah.

With over thirty years of experience as a marriage and individual therapist Karen currently serves as a private practitioner working with a broad spectrum of individual and corporate clients. She has done extensive work with individuals in all types and phases of relationships and has spent the last decade focused on helping clients architect better relationships – whether they are just starting out, newly divorced and getting back in the dating game, or have been married for years.

Karen is an interactive, solution-focused therapist. Her approach is to provide support and practical feedback to help clients effectively address personal life challenges. She integrates complementary methodologies and techniques to offer a highly personalized approach tailored to each client. Using her extensive experience with Myers-Briggs personality inventory she helps clients build on their strengths and attain the personal growth they are committed to accomplishing.

Karen holds a masters degree in social work and a bachelor's degree in psychology from the University of Utah.

Natalie House

Natalie House has spent over twenty years in marketing at high-tech companies. Natalie was referred to Karen when she was going through her divorce and she likes to say that when she met Karen she couldn't find her way out of a paper bag. Karen gave her the tools to know herself, love herself, transform herself and transform her relationships with friends, family, colleagues and her partner.

What Natalie loves about Karen's methodology is that Karen has made mindfulness easier and more approachable. It's practical, pragmatic, honest and focused on what can be done in the here and now that will change your life in the long run.

Natalie's goal is to use her marketing experience to make Karen's concepts accessible to as many people as possible. Natalie is living proof that if you do the work, you will change your life.

Natalie holds a Master of Business Administration and a bachelor's degree in business from the University of Phoenix.

Notes:

Lightning Source UK Ltd.
Milton Keynes UK
UKHW020958101019
351279UK00010B/129/P